KATHERINE AHARON

She Rises with Strength

Daily Devotional for Women 2025

Contents

Introduction v

1 Day 1: Anchored in Christ 1

2 Day 2: God's Word in Uncertain Times 3

3 Day 3: Embracing God's Unchanging Love 5

4 Day 4: Walking in Grace Amid Mistakes 7

5 Day 5: Overcoming the Fear of Failure 9

6 Day 6: Rest for the Anxious Heart 11

7 Day 7: Trusting God's Timing in Life's Transitions 13

8 Day 8: Strength in the Face of Weakness 15

9 Day 9: God's Provision in Financial Struggles 17

10 Day 10: Finding Joy in the Mundane 19

11 Day 11: Letting Go of Perfectionism 21

12 Day 12: Managing Stress with God's Peace 23

13 Day 13: Overcoming the Fear of the Unknown 25

14 Day 14: God's Comfort in Loneliness 27

15 Day 15: A Light to the World 29

16 Day 16: Overcoming Comparison 31

17 Day 17: Balancing Work, Family, and Faith 33

18 Day 18: Healing from Past Hurts 35

19 Day 19: Breaking Free from Worry 37

20 Day 20: Finding Hope After Loss 39

21 Day 21: Battling Negative Self-Talk 41

22 Day 22: Freedom from Guilt and Shame 43

23 Day 23: Cultivating a Grateful Heart 45

24 Day 24: Pressing Through Burnout 47

25 Day 25: God's Faithfulness Through Life's Storms 49

26 Day 26: Love and Boundaries   51

27 Day 27: Building Relationships Rooted in Christ   53

28 Day 28: Finding Purpose in Every Season   55

29 Day 29: Sharing Your Story with Boldness   57

30 Day 30: Living a Life of Victory   59

31 Closing Reflection and Prayer   61

Introduction

Hello, and welcome to *Daily Devotional for Women*!

I'm so glad you're here, holding this book in your hands. Whether you're flipping through these pages out of curiosity, looking for a way to reconnect with God, or hoping for some encouragement in your daily life, you've come to the right place. This devotional isn't just about reading words on a page—it's about creating space for God to meet you, speak to you, and walk with you every day.

Life can feel like a whirlwind, can't it? Between the responsibilities we juggle and the expectations we carry, it's easy to feel overwhelmed or even disconnected from God. Maybe you've struggled to find time for prayer or reading Scripture. Maybe you've wondered if God is still listening. Or maybe you're simply hungry for more of Him in your life. Wherever you are right now—spiritually, emotionally, and physically—this devotional is here to meet you, right where you are.

You don't need to be perfect to come to God. You don't need to have all the answers or get everything "right." All He asks is that you show up. And that's what this book is all about: helping you show up every day to spend time with Him, even in the smallest moments.

Each day's devotion is short and simple—just a few minutes of Scripture, reflection, and prayer. Think of it as a daily conversation with God, a moment to pause, reset, and refocus on what matters most. Some days, the words will challenge you. Other days, they'll comfort you. But every day, they'll point you back to the truth of God's love, faithfulness, and presence in your life.

You might be wondering, "Why do I need a daily devotional? Can't I just pray or read the Bible on my own?" Absolutely, you can—and I hope you do! But there's something powerful about having a consistent rhythm of spending time with God. It's like watering a garden. The more time you invest in His Word, the more your faith grows, blooms, and bears fruit.

Daily devotions help us stay anchored when life feels chaotic. They remind us of God's promises when we're tempted to doubt. They give us strength when we're weary and joy when we feel empty. Most importantly, they remind us that we're not walking through life alone.

This devotional is for you—the woman who's seeking, striving, or simply surviving. It's for the woman who wants to deepen her faith, rediscover her purpose, or just take a breath in God's presence. It's for the woman who feels strong one day and unsure the next. And it's for the woman who needs to be reminded of this truth: You are deeply loved by God, just as you are.

As you journey through this book, know that you're not alone. Women all over the world are opening these same pages, seeking the same God, and drawing from the same well of grace. We may have different stories, but we share the same hope—that God's Word will transform us, one day at a time.

So, let's do this together. Let's commit to showing up, even on the hard days. Let's lean into His love, trust His timing, and grow in faith as we walk through this year.

1

Day 1: Anchored in Christ

"We have this hope as an anchor for the soul, firm and secure. It enters the inner sanctuary behind the curtain."
Hebrews 6:19

Life is full of unexpected storms. Challenges at work, pressures at home, or even personal doubts can leave you feeling adrift. In these moments, it's easy to grasp at temporary solutions—success, approval, or control. Yet these things fail to steady us when the winds of life blow hardest.

The good news is that as believers, we have a steadfast anchor: Jesus Christ. Anchors serve a single purpose—to keep a vessel steady and secure, no matter the strength of the storm. Similarly, Christ offers us stability and hope when life feels overwhelming. His promises never waver, and His love remains constant.

When you place your faith in Him, you are no longer tossed by the waves of uncertainty or fear. Instead, you are tethered to something unshakable—an eternal hope that sustains you in every season of life.

Reflect

- What storms are you facing right now that make you feel unsteady?

- In what ways have you relied on temporary "anchors" instead of Christ?
- How can you remind yourself daily that Jesus is your source of hope and stability?

Prayer

Heavenly Father, thank You for being my anchor in the storms of life. Help me to trust in Your unchanging promises and to hold fast to the hope I have in Jesus. When I feel overwhelmed, remind me that You are my refuge, my strength, and my firm foundation. Keep me anchored in Your love, no matter what comes my way. In Jesus' name, Amen.

Action Step

Write down three promises of God that you can cling to when life feels uncertain. Place them somewhere visible as a daily reminder of your anchor in Christ.

Promise to Hold On To

"God is our refuge and strength, an ever-present help in trouble." —Psalm 46:1

2

Day 2: God's Word in Uncertain Times

"Your word is a lamp to my feet and a light to my path."
Psalm 119:105

Life's uncertainties can feel like walking through a dark forest without a flashlight. Questions swirl in your mind: What decision should I make? What's next for my family? How do I navigate this difficult situation? During these moments of confusion, God's Word becomes your guiding light, illuminating the next step forward.

The Bible isn't just a book of ancient stories; it's alive and active, offering wisdom, comfort, and clarity for every situation. When fear and doubt threaten to overwhelm you, turning to God's Word provides reassurance and direction.

The beauty of Scripture is that it doesn't always reveal the entire path ahead—it often provides just enough light for the step you're on. This encourages you to walk in faith, trusting that God will guide you as you continue to seek Him.

In uncertain times, remember that God's Word is your unchanging compass in an ever-changing world. Meditate on His promises, and let His truth replace your anxiety with peace and confidence.

Reflect

- What decisions or situations in your life feel unclear right now?
- How can you make Scripture a part of your daily routine to help navigate uncertainty?
- Is there a specific Bible verse or passage that has brought you peace in the past?

Prayer

Lord, thank You for the gift of Your Word. In times of uncertainty, help me to seek Your guidance and trust the truth of Scripture. When I feel lost or unsure, remind me to rely on the promises You've given me. Let Your Word be my light and my guide, giving me peace as I follow Your will. In Jesus' name, Amen.

Action Step

Choose one verse or passage that speaks to your current struggles or uncertainties. Write it down and reflect on it throughout the day. Let it be a source of encouragement and direction for you.

Promise to Hold On To

"Trust in the Lord with all your heart and lean not on your own understanding; in all your ways submit to him, and he will make your paths straight." —Proverbs 3:5-6

3

Day 3: Embracing God's Unchanging Love

"For I am convinced that neither death nor life, neither angels nor demons, neither the present nor the future, nor any powers, neither height nor depth, nor anything else in all creation, will be able to separate us from the love of God that is in Christ Jesus our Lord."
Romans 8:38-39

Relationships evolve, seasons shift, and the things we once held dear can fade away. This uncertainty can sometimes make us question our worth or wonder if we are truly loved. But God's love is unlike anything else. It is constant, unwavering, and unconditional.

In a world where love often feels conditional—based on achievements, appearance, or performance—God's love stands as a firm foundation. He loves you not because of what you do, but because of who He is. His love doesn't fluctuate with your failures or grow stronger with your successes. It is the same yesterday, today, and forever.

When you embrace the truth of God's unchanging love, you can let go of the pressure to earn His approval. You can rest in the assurance that nothing—not your past mistakes, your present struggles, or your future fears—can separate you from Him.

Let His love be the anchor for your heart and the peace for your soul. Embrace it, live in it, and let it transform the way you see yourself and the world around you.

Reflect

- Are there areas of your life where you feel unworthy of God's love?
- How does knowing that God's love is unchanging bring peace to your heart?
- How can you live differently today, knowing that you are fully loved by God?

Prayer

Heavenly Father, thank You for loving me with an unchanging, unconditional love. Help me to let go of striving for approval and rest in the truth that I am fully accepted by You. When doubts creep in, remind me of Your promises and the unshakable truth of Your love. Let Your love shape my heart and my life. In Jesus' name, Amen.

Action Step

Take five minutes today to meditate on God's love for you. Write down three ways His love has shown up in your life recently. Keep this list as a reminder of His faithfulness.

Promise to Hold On To

"The steadfast love of the Lord never ceases; His mercies never come to an end; they are new every morning; great is Your faithfulness." —Lamentations 3:22-23

4

Day 4: Walking in Grace Amid Mistakes

"For it is by grace you have been saved, through faith—and this is not from yourselves, it is the gift of God."
Ephesians 2:8

Mistakes are part of the human experience. Sometimes they're small missteps; other times, they feel monumental, weighing us down with guilt and regret. But no matter the size of our mistakes, God's grace is greater. His forgiveness is not something you earn through good behavior or trying harder—it's a free gift, given out of His boundless love for you.

Accepting God's forgiveness means releasing yourself from the burden of shame and trusting in the finished work of Christ on the cross. Grace reminds you that your mistakes don't define you; your identity is rooted in being a beloved child of God.

Walking in grace doesn't mean you'll never stumble again. It means that when you do, you can confidently approach God, knowing He is faithful to forgive and restore. With His grace, you can learn from your mistakes, grow in humility, and move forward without fear or condemnation.

Let today be the day you stop holding on to past mistakes. God's grace invites you to start fresh, empowered by His love and forgiveness.

Reflect

- What mistakes or regrets are you struggling to let go of?
- How does knowing that God's grace is a gift change the way you view forgiveness?
- In what ways can you show yourself the same grace God has shown you?

Prayer

Lord, thank You for the incredible gift of grace. I come to You with my mistakes, trusting in Your forgiveness and love. Help me to release the burdens of guilt and shame and to walk forward in the freedom that only You can give. Teach me to extend grace to myself and others, reflecting Your mercy in my life. In Jesus' name, Amen.

Action Step

Take a moment to write down one mistake or regret you've been holding on to. Pray over it, asking God for forgiveness. Then tear up the paper as a symbol of releasing it to Him and accepting His grace.

Promise to Hold On To

"If we confess our sins, he is faithful and just and will forgive us our sins and purify us from all unrighteousness." —1 John 1:9

5

Day 5: Overcoming the Fear of Failure

"For the Spirit God gave us does not make us timid, but gives us power, love, and self-discipline."
2 Timothy 1:7

Failure is a fear that grips many of us. It whispers, "You're not enough," "You'll never succeed," or "What if you make a mistake?" This fear can keep you paralyzed, preventing you from stepping into the life God has for you. But God's Word reminds us that fear is not from Him. Instead, He gives us a spirit of power, love, and self-discipline to face challenges with courage and faith.

God doesn't expect you to navigate life's challenges perfectly. He calls you to trust Him and take the next step in faith, knowing that even if you stumble, He will guide and sustain you. The fear of failure loses its grip when you shift your focus from your own abilities to God's promises and power.

When you trust that God is with you, you can embrace challenges as opportunities to grow and depend on Him. He doesn't measure your worth by your successes or failures—He values your willingness to step forward in obedience. Failure isn't the end; it's often the doorway to deeper dependence on Him and greater purpose in your life.

Reflect

- What fears or doubts are holding you back from stepping out in faith?
- How can trusting God's guidance give you courage to face challenges?
- Think of a time when failure taught you something valuable. How did God use that experience for your growth?

Prayer

Lord, thank You for reminding me that fear is not from You. When I feel overwhelmed by the fear of failure, help me to trust in Your power and promises. Teach me to see challenges as opportunities to rely on You and to grow in faith. Strengthen me with courage and give me the discipline to take each step forward in obedience. In Jesus' name, Amen.

Action Step

Write down one challenge or goal you've been avoiding because of the fear of failure. Pray over it and ask God for the courage to take one step forward today, trusting Him with the outcome.

Promise to Hold On To

"Be strong and courageous. Do not be afraid; do not be discouraged, for the Lord your God will be with you wherever you go." —Joshua 1:9

6

Day 6: Rest for the Anxious Heart

"Come to me, all you who are weary and burdened, and I will give you rest. Take my yoke upon you and learn from me, for I am gentle and humble in heart, and you will find rest for your souls. For my yoke is easy and my burden is light."
Matthew 11:28-30

Anxiety has a way of gripping your heart, leaving you overwhelmed and restless. The pressures of life—deadlines, relationships, finances—can weigh so heavily that peace feels out of reach. But in the midst of the chaos, Jesus extends a tender invitation: **"Come to me."**

His invitation is not to a life free of challenges but to a life where you don't carry those burdens alone. When you surrender your stress to Him, you exchange the weight of your worries for the lightness of His grace. Jesus doesn't demand perfection; He offers rest for your soul through His gentle and humble heart.

Resting in Christ doesn't mean ignoring your responsibilities—it means trusting Him to equip you with the strength and wisdom to face them. When you place your anxieties in His hands, you make room for His peace to settle in your heart.

You were never meant to carry life's burdens alone. Let today be the day you lay them down at His feet and embrace the rest He promises.

Reflect

- What burdens or stresses are weighing on your heart right now?
- How does trusting Jesus with your anxieties bring peace to your soul?
- What steps can you take today to surrender your worries to God?

Prayer

Jesus, I come to You today with my anxious heart. I lay my burdens at Your feet, trusting You to carry what I cannot. Teach me to rest in Your presence and to rely on Your strength instead of my own. Replace my worries with Your peace and remind me that You are always in control. Thank You for being my refuge and my rest. In Your name, Amen.

Action Step

Take five minutes to sit quietly in prayer, visualizing yourself placing each worry or burden into God's hands. As you do, breathe deeply and reflect on His promise to give you rest.

Promise to Hold On To

"Cast all your anxiety on him because he cares for you." —1 Peter 5:7

7

Day 7: Trusting God's Timing in Life's Transitions

"He has made everything beautiful in its time. He has also set eternity in the human heart; yet no one can fathom what God has done from beginning to end."
Ecclesiastes 3:11

Life's transitions can be both exciting and unsettling. Whether you're navigating a career change, a shift in family dynamics, or uncertainty in relationships, waiting for clarity can feel like wandering in a fog. You may wonder if God sees your struggles or if His plans will ever unfold.

Ecclesiastes reminds us that God's timing is perfect, even when we can't see the full picture. He has a plan for every season, and in His wisdom, He makes all things beautiful in their time—not ours. Trusting His timing requires faith, patience, and a surrender of your own expectations.

When transitions make you feel out of control, remember that God is never hurried or delayed. He knows exactly where you are and where you're going. Instead of striving to force outcomes, lean into His guidance and trust that He's working behind the scenes. While the waiting may feel difficult, it's often where God refines and prepares you for what's ahead.

Let go of the anxiety of trying to figure it all out. Rest in the truth that God is faithful and will make everything beautiful in its perfect time.

Reflect

- What transitions are you currently navigating, and how are they challenging your faith?
- How does trusting in God's timing bring peace during seasons of uncertainty?
- In what ways can you surrender your timeline to God and embrace His plan?

Prayer

Lord, thank You for reminding me that Your timing is always perfect. In the midst of life's transitions, help me to trust You fully and surrender my own plans to Your greater purpose. Teach me patience and give me the faith to rest in Your promises. Remind me that You are always working for my good, even when I can't see it. In Jesus' name, Amen.

Action Step

Write down a situation where you feel anxious about timing (career, family, or relationships). Pray over it, asking God to give you peace and clarity. Then release it to Him, trusting that He will make all things beautiful in His time.

Promise to Hold On To

"The Lord is not slow in keeping his promise, as some understand slowness. Instead, he is patient with you, not wanting anyone to perish, but everyone to come to repentance." —2 Peter 3:9

8

Day 8: Strength in the Face of Weakness

"But he said to me, 'My grace is sufficient for you, for my power is made perfect in weakness.' Therefore I will boast all the more gladly about my weaknesses, so that Christ's power may rest on me."
2 Corinthians 12:9

There are days when the weight of life leaves you feeling completely depleted—emotionally, physically, or spiritually. You may find yourself wondering how you'll keep going when your strength is gone. The truth is, moments of weakness are not a sign of failure but an opportunity to experience God's power in a profound way.

Paul's words in 2 Corinthians 12:9 remind us that God's grace is not just sufficient; it's transformative. In your moments of exhaustion and vulnerability, His power becomes evident. Rather than hiding your weakness or pushing through on your own, you can invite God into your struggle and allow His strength to sustain you.

Relying on God means admitting that you don't have to do it all on your own. It's an act of humility and faith to lean on His promises instead of your own abilities. When you are emotionally drained, let His presence be your refuge and His Word your source of renewal.

God doesn't ask you to be strong on your own—He invites you to find strength in Him. Trust that His power is enough to carry you through even the hardest days.

Reflect

- What situations in your life are leaving you emotionally or spiritually drained?
- How can you remind yourself to turn to God instead of relying on your own strength?
- What does it mean to you that God's power is made perfect in your weakness?

Prayer

Lord, I feel so drained and weak today, but I know Your grace is sufficient for me. Help me to rely on Your strength and not my own. Teach me to find peace in my limitations, knowing that Your power is made perfect in my weakness. Thank You for being my refuge and my source of strength. In Jesus' name, Amen.

Action Step

Take a moment to identify one area where you feel emotionally drained. Write a short prayer surrendering it to God, asking for His strength and grace to carry you through.

Promise to Hold On To

"The Lord gives strength to his people; the Lord blesses his people with peace."
—Psalm 29:11

9

Day 9: God's Provision in Financial Struggles

"And my God will meet all your needs according to the riches of his glory in Christ Jesus."
Philippians 4:19

Financial struggles can stir up anxiety, frustration, and fear. The uncertainty of how you'll cover bills or provide for your family can weigh heavily on your heart. But God's promise in Philippians 4:19 reminds us that He is not just aware of your needs—He is fully capable of meeting them.

God's provision may not always come in the way you expect, but He is faithful to supply what you truly need. Sometimes, His provision looks like unexpected opportunities, the generosity of others, or even a deeper contentment that allows you to see abundance in the midst of scarcity.

Trusting God in financial struggles requires surrendering your fears and embracing His promises. It means acknowledging that He is your ultimate provider, not your paycheck or savings account. As you place your trust in Him, He will guide your steps, give you wisdom in managing your resources, and remind you that His riches are far greater than material wealth.

No matter what your financial situation looks like today, trust that God sees you, cares for you, and will meet your needs in His perfect way and timing.

Reflect

- What financial struggles are you currently facing, and how have they affected your faith?
- How can you practice gratitude and trust in God's provision, even during challenging times?
- In what ways can you seek God's wisdom in managing your resources?

Prayer

Father, I thank You for being my provider. In the midst of financial struggles, help me to trust in Your faithfulness and provision. Calm my anxious heart and give me the wisdom to make wise decisions with what You've entrusted to me. Remind me that You are my source and that Your riches in glory far exceed my earthly needs. Thank You for always caring for me. In Jesus' name, Amen.

Action Step

Write down three ways God has provided for you in the past, no matter how small. Reflect on these moments as reminders of His faithfulness, and thank Him for His ongoing provision.

Promise to Hold On To

"The young lions suffer want and hunger; but those who seek the Lord lack no good thing." —Psalm 34:10

10

Day 10: Finding Joy in the Mundane

"Whatever you do, work at it with all your heart, as working for the Lord, not for human masters."
Colossians 3:23

Life is often filled with mundane tasks—dishes to wash, errands to run, emails to answer, and chores that seem never-ending. It's easy to feel as though the day-to-day grind has no meaning. But God's Word reminds us that even the smallest actions can carry eternal significance when done for Him.

Colossians 3:23 teaches us that our work, no matter how ordinary, is an opportunity to glorify God. When you approach your daily routine with a heart of gratitude and service, you can transform mundane moments into acts of worship. Whether it's preparing meals for your family, completing a project at work, or simply showing kindness to a stranger, these seemingly small actions reflect God's love and faithfulness.

Finding joy in the mundane doesn't mean every task will suddenly feel exciting, but it does mean that your perspective can change. When you choose to focus on how your work honors God and serves others, you'll discover a deeper sense of purpose and fulfillment in even the most routine activities.

Reflect

- What daily tasks or routines feel especially mundane or unimportant to you?
- How can shifting your perspective help you see these tasks as opportunities to glorify God?
- What small step can you take today to infuse more joy and purpose into your routine?

Prayer

Lord, thank You for the reminder that even the smallest tasks can glorify You. Help me to approach my daily routine with a heart of gratitude and purpose. Teach me to see every moment as an opportunity to serve You and reflect Your love. Transform my perspective, and fill me with joy as I do my work for Your glory. In Jesus' name, Amen.

Action Step

Choose one mundane task you often find frustrating or boring. As you complete it today, pray over it and thank God for the opportunity to serve Him in that moment.

Promise to Hold On To

"So whether you eat or drink or whatever you do, do it all for the glory of God."
—1 Corinthians 10:31

11

Day 11: Letting Go of Perfectionism

"I praise you because I am fearfully and wonderfully made; your works are wonderful, I know that full well."
Psalm 139:14

Perfectionism whispers lies that you must always achieve more, do better, and meet impossible standards to be worthy. It can leave you exhausted, frustrated, and feeling like you'll never measure up. But God didn't create you to chase perfection—He created you to live in freedom, resting in His grace and celebrating the beauty of your God-given uniqueness.

Psalm 139:14 reminds us that we are fearfully and wonderfully made. You are God's masterpiece, crafted with care and intention. He didn't design you to fit a mold or meet the world's expectations but to reflect His glory in the unique way only you can.

When you let go of perfectionism, you create space to embrace who God made you to be. You begin to value progress over perfection, growth over guilt, and grace over striving. God's love for you is not based on flawless performance but on His unchanging nature and the work of Christ on the cross.

Release the burden of trying to be "perfect" and instead rest in the truth that you are already enough in God's eyes. Live confidently, knowing that His grace covers your imperfections and His power is made perfect in your weakness.

Reflect

- In what areas of your life are you striving for perfection, and how is it affecting you?
- How does knowing you are fearfully and wonderfully made help you let go of impossible standards?
- What steps can you take to replace perfectionism with grace and gratitude?

Prayer

Lord, thank You for creating me in Your image and for reminding me that I am fearfully and wonderfully made. Help me to let go of perfectionism and the pressure to meet impossible standards. Teach me to rest in Your grace and to embrace my God-given uniqueness. Thank You for loving me just as I am and for walking with me as I grow. In Jesus' name, Amen.

Action Step

Write down one area where you've been striving for perfection. Beside it, write a truth about how God sees you (e.g., "I am loved" or "I am enough in Christ"). Read it aloud daily to replace the lie of perfectionism with God's truth.

Promise to Hold On To

"But he said to me, 'My grace is sufficient for you, for my power is made perfect in weakness.' Therefore I will boast all the more gladly about my weaknesses, so that Christ's power may rest on me." —2 Corinthians 12:9

12

Day 12: Managing Stress with God's Peace

"Do not be anxious about anything, but in every situation, by prayer and petition, with thanksgiving, present your requests to God. And the peace of God, which transcends all understanding, will guard your hearts and your minds in Christ Jesus."
Philippians 4:6-7

Stress can often feel like a constant companion in life, creeping into your thoughts and stealing your peace. The demands of work, family, and daily responsibilities can overwhelm even the strongest heart. But God offers you a better way: His peace that surpasses all understanding.

In Philippians 4:6-7, Paul encourages us to respond to stress not with worry, but with prayer. Instead of trying to control everything, we're invited to release our burdens to God. When you surrender your anxieties to Him in prayer, coupled with thanksgiving, you open the door for His peace to flood your heart and mind.

This peace doesn't come from having all the answers or seeing your circumstances change immediately. It comes from trusting that God is in control and that His plans for you are good. When you place your trust in Him, your stress begins to lose its grip, replaced by the calm assurance that God is working in every detail of your life.

Let today be the day you choose to release control and rest in the perfect

23

peace that only God can provide.

Reflect

- What situations in your life are causing you the most stress right now?
- How can prayer and thanksgiving help you release control and trust God?
- What does it mean for you to experience God's peace that transcends all understanding?

Prayer

Lord, I come to You today with a heart weighed down by stress. I release my worries and anxieties into Your hands, trusting that You are in control. Teach me to pray with thanksgiving, even when I feel overwhelmed. Fill my heart and mind with Your peace, and remind me that You are working for my good in every situation. Thank You for being my refuge and strength. In Jesus' name, Amen.

Action Step

Set aside 10 minutes today to pray over the specific stresses in your life. As you pray, thank God for His faithfulness and His presence, trusting Him to handle what you cannot.

Promise to Hold On To

"Cast your cares on the Lord and he will sustain you; he will never let the righteous be shaken." —Psalm 55:22

13

Day 13: Overcoming the Fear of the Unknown

"So do not fear, for I am with you; do not be dismayed, for I am your God. I will strengthen you and help you; I will uphold you with my righteous right hand."
Isaiah 41:10

The fear of the unknown can feel paralyzing. What will happen next? Will things work out? Uncertainty about the future can lead to worry, doubt, and sleepless nights. But Isaiah 41:10 reminds us of a powerful truth: God is with you.

When you face the unknown, you don't walk alone. God promises to strengthen, help, and uphold you, no matter what lies ahead. While you may not know the future, you can rest in the fact that God holds it in His hands. He sees the path before you and has a plan that is far greater than anything you could imagine.

Faith doesn't mean ignoring your fears; it means facing them with the confidence that God is in control. Instead of allowing uncertainty to overwhelm you, lean into His promises. Trust that He is working all things together for your good and His glory, even when the way forward seems unclear.

The unknown can be intimidating, but it's also an opportunity to grow in trust and dependence on God. Take His hand, step forward, and rest in His unshakable presence.

Reflect

- What uncertainties in your life are causing you fear or hesitation?
- How does Isaiah 41:10 reassure you of God's presence and strength in uncertain times?
- What steps can you take today to release your fear and trust God's plan?

Prayer

Lord, You know the fears that arise in my heart when I face the unknown. Help me to trust in Your promises and to lean on Your strength instead of my own. Thank You for being with me in every situation, for upholding me, and for guiding my steps. Fill me with peace and confidence as I walk forward in faith, knowing that You have a good plan for my life. In Jesus' name, Amen.

Action Step

Write down one area of uncertainty in your life. Beside it, write this promise: *"God is with me and will strengthen me."* Pray over this situation, declaring your trust in God's plan and releasing your fears into His hands.

Promise to Hold On To

"For I know the plans I have for you," declares the Lord, "plans to prosper you and not to harm you, plans to give you hope and a future." —Jeremiah 29:11

14

Day 14: God's Comfort in Loneliness

"The Lord is close to the brokenhearted and saves those who are crushed in spirit."
Psalm 34:18

Loneliness can weigh heavily on your soul, leaving you feeling unseen and unloved. Whether it's the loss of a relationship, a season of isolation, or simply feeling misunderstood, loneliness has a way of making the world feel empty. But in the midst of it, God offers you His comforting presence.

Psalm 34:18 reminds us that the Lord is near to the brokenhearted. He doesn't stand at a distance or wait for you to "get over it." Instead, He comes close, offering His peace and love when you feel most alone. This intimacy with God is a reminder that, no matter what your circumstances may look like, you are never truly alone.

Loneliness can be an invitation to draw nearer to God. It's in these quiet moments that you can hear His voice, feel His embrace, and be reminded of His promises. As you pour out your heart to Him in prayer, you'll discover that He understands your pain and is faithful to meet you right where you are.

God is your refuge in loneliness. Trust Him to fill the empty spaces in your heart with His love and comfort.

Reflect

- What has been your greatest struggle in times of loneliness?
- How can you use moments of isolation to deepen your relationship with God?
- What does it mean to you that God is close to the brokenhearted?

Prayer

Lord, thank You for being near to me when I feel alone. In moments of loneliness, remind me of Your presence and fill my heart with Your peace. Teach me to lean on You and to find joy and intimacy in our relationship. Help me to trust that You are working even in the quiet seasons of my life. Thank You for Your love that never leaves or forsakes me. In Jesus' name, Amen.

Action Step

Set aside 15 minutes today to sit in God's presence. Share your feelings of loneliness with Him in prayer, and then listen for His still, small voice. Write down any scriptures, thoughts, or impressions He places on your heart.

Promise to Hold On To

"Never will I leave you; never will I forsake you." —Hebrews 13:5

15

Day 15: A Light to the World

"You are the light of the world. A town built on a hill cannot be hidden. Neither do people light a lamp and put it under a bowl. Instead, they put it on its stand, and it gives light to everyone in the house. In the same way, let your light shine before others, that they may see your good deeds and glorify your Father in heaven."
Matthew 5:14-16

In a world often filled with darkness—fear, division, and uncertainty—God calls you to be a light. Your life, infused with His presence, is a beacon of hope and love to those around you. Being a light doesn't mean being perfect; it means allowing God to shine through your words, actions, and attitudes.

Jesus reminds us in Matthew 5:14-16 that as His followers, we are not meant to hide our faith but to live it out boldly and authentically. Your everyday actions—showing kindness to a coworker, comforting a friend, or standing up for what's right—can point others to God's love.

The light you carry is not your own; it's a reflection of the One who has transformed you. By staying close to God through prayer, His Word, and worship, you allow His light to shine brighter in your life. Even when you feel small or insignificant, remember that a single candle can illuminate a dark room.

Let your life be a testimony of God's love, grace, and hope. As you shine

His light, you glorify Him and draw others to the truth of His presence.

Reflect

- How can you reflect God's love in your daily interactions?
- What "bowls" (fears, insecurities, distractions) might be hiding your light from shining brightly?
- How can you intentionally shine God's light in a specific area of your life today?

Prayer

Lord, thank You for calling me to be a light in this world. Help me to reflect Your love and grace in my words and actions. Remove anything in my life that dims Your light, and give me the courage to live out my faith boldly. Let others see You through me and be drawn to Your goodness. Thank You for the privilege of being part of Your plan to bring hope and light to the world. In Jesus' name, Amen.

Action Step

Identify one practical way to reflect God's love today—whether it's helping someone in need, sharing an encouraging word, or offering forgiveness. Take that step with the intention of glorifying God.

Promise to Hold On To

"The light shines in the darkness, and the darkness has not overcome it." —John 1:5

16

Day 16: Overcoming Comparison

*"Each one should test their own actions. Then they can take pride in themselves
alone, without comparing themselves to someone else, for each one should carry
their own load."*
Galatians 6:4-5

Comparison is a thief of joy. It can lead you to focus on what others
have, what they've accomplished, or who they appear to be, leaving
you feeling inadequate or envious. But God never intended for you
to measure your worth by the standards of others.

In Galatians 6:4-5, Paul reminds us to test our own actions and to take
responsibility for our unique journey. God has created you with specific gifts,
a distinct purpose, and a path that is different from anyone else's. When you
shift your focus from what others are doing to what God is doing in you,
you'll find freedom and contentment.

Overcoming comparison begins with gratitude. Instead of longing for
someone else's blessings, thank God for the ones He's already given you.
Celebrate your strengths and trust that God's plan for your life is perfect.
When you embrace who God made you to be, you'll experience the joy and
peace that come from living authentically in His purpose.

You were never meant to be like anyone else—you were meant to reflect
God's glory in your unique way.

Reflect

- In what areas of your life do you find yourself comparing yourself to others?
- How can gratitude help you overcome feelings of inadequacy or envy?
- What is one step you can take to focus more on God's plan for your life and less on others' journeys?

Prayer

Lord, forgive me for the times I've compared myself to others and doubted my worth. Help me to see myself through Your eyes and to trust in the unique purpose You have for my life. Teach me to be content with who You've made me to be and to celebrate the blessings You've given me. Thank You for creating me with intention and for guiding me each step of the way. In Jesus' name, Amen.

Action Step

Take time today to write a list of 10 blessings or strengths you're thankful for in your own life. When the urge to compare arises, revisit this list and thank God for how He's working in and through you.

Promise to Hold On To

"For we are God's handiwork, created in Christ Jesus to do good works, which God prepared in advance for us to do." —Ephesians 2:10

17

Day 17: Balancing Work, Family, and Faith

"She watches over the affairs of her household and does not eat the bread of idleness."
Proverbs 31:27

Balancing the many demands of work, family, and faith can feel overwhelming. The pressure to excel in all areas often leaves you feeling stretched thin, exhausted, and unsure if you're doing enough. But God never intended for you to carry this weight alone. He invites you to seek His wisdom and strength as you navigate life's demands.

The woman in Proverbs 31 is often seen as the ultimate example of a balanced life. She cares for her household, works diligently, and honors God in all she does. Yet her ability to balance everything doesn't come from her own strength—it comes from her deep dependence on God.

Balancing work, family, and faith starts with prioritizing your relationship with God. When you place Him at the center, He gives you the clarity to focus on what truly matters. Some seasons may require more attention to your family, while others might demand a greater focus on work. Seeking God's wisdom daily allows you to embrace these shifts with grace.

Remember, balance doesn't mean perfection. It means being faithful with what God has entrusted to you and trusting Him to fill the gaps where you fall short.

Reflect

- What area of your life feels most overwhelming right now, and have you sought God's guidance for it?
- How can placing God at the center of your day help you better balance your responsibilities?
- What steps can you take to create space for rest and spiritual renewal in your busy schedule?

Prayer

Lord, I bring the demands of my life before You, knowing that I can't balance everything on my own. Give me wisdom to prioritize what truly matters and strength to handle each task with grace. Help me to trust in Your guidance and to honor You in my work, my family, and my faith. Thank You for being my source of peace and for walking with me in every season. In Jesus' name, Amen.

Action Step

Take 10 minutes to review your daily schedule. Identify one task you can delegate, one you can postpone, and one way you can intentionally spend time with God.

Promise to Hold On To

"Commit to the Lord whatever you do, and he will establish your plans."
—Proverbs 16:3

18

Day 18: Healing from Past Hurts

"He heals the brokenhearted and binds up their wounds."
Psalm 147:3

Life can leave scars. Disappointments, betrayals, and painful memories can linger in your heart, making it hard to move forward. Sometimes, you may feel like the wounds are too deep to heal. But Psalm 147:3 is a beautiful reminder of God's tender care—He is the ultimate healer of broken hearts.

Healing from past hurts doesn't mean ignoring the pain or pretending it didn't happen. It means bringing your wounds to God, the One who knows your pain and loves you deeply. He longs to mend what is broken, restoring your heart and giving you hope for the future.

As you surrender your hurts to God, trust His timing. Healing is often a process, not an instant transformation. Spend time in prayer, pour out your emotions to Him, and meditate on His Word. Surround yourself with people who encourage you and remind you of God's faithfulness.

The journey of healing is not just about letting go of the past; it's about embracing the new life God has for you. Trust Him to make beauty out of your brokenness, for His plans for you are always for your good.

Reflect

- What past hurts are you still carrying, and have you brought them before God?
- How can trusting in God's love and care help you release the pain of the past?
- What steps can you take to allow God's healing process to begin or continue?

Prayer

Lord, You see the wounds I carry, the hurts that weigh heavy on my heart. I bring them to You today, trusting in Your promise to heal and restore me. Mend what is broken and help me to let go of bitterness, fear, and pain. Fill my heart with Your peace and teach me to trust Your plan for my life. Thank You for being the healer of my heart and the restorer of my soul. In Jesus' name, Amen.

Action Step

Write down one past hurt that you've been holding onto. Pray over it, asking God to help you release the pain and begin the healing process. Consider sharing your journey with a trusted friend or counselor.

Promise to Hold On To

"The Lord is close to the brokenhearted and saves those who are crushed in spirit."
—Psalm 34:18

19

Day 19: Breaking Free from Worry

*"Therefore do not worry about tomorrow, for tomorrow will worry about itself.
Each day has enough trouble of its own."*
Matthew 6:34

Worry often creeps into your mind without warning. It can dominate your thoughts, leaving you consumed by "what-ifs" and worst-case scenarios. But Jesus invites you to a life free from worry—a life of trust and peace.

In Matthew 6:34, Jesus reminds us to focus on today. Worrying about tomorrow doesn't change what will happen; it only steals the joy and peace God intends for you in the present. Trusting God one day at a time means believing that He is in control, no matter what the future holds.

Breaking free from worry starts with surrender. When anxious thoughts arise, bring them to God in prayer. Declare His promises over your situation and choose to focus on His faithfulness. Let gratitude fill your heart as you remember the ways He has provided for you in the past.

God's grace is sufficient for today. You don't need to have all the answers or fix every problem. Rest in the assurance that God holds your tomorrow and is walking with you today.

Reflect

- What situations in your life tend to make you worry the most?
- How can trusting God for today help you let go of concerns about the future?
- What is one way you can practice surrendering your worries to God?

Prayer

Lord, I confess that I often allow worry to take over my thoughts. Help me to trust You fully, one day at a time. Remind me that You are in control of my life and that Your grace is enough for today. Give me peace and strengthen my faith as I surrender my anxieties to You. Thank You for walking with me and for being my refuge in every season. In Jesus' name, Amen.

Action Step

Each time a worry comes to mind today, pause and say, "Lord, I give this to You." Write down the worries you release to God, and at the end of the day, thank Him for His peace and provision.

Promise to Hold On To

"Cast all your anxiety on him because he cares for you." —1 Peter 5:7

20

Day 20: Finding Hope After Loss

"He will wipe every tear from their eyes. There will be no more death' or mourning or crying or pain, for the old order of things has passed away."
Revelation 21:4

Loss is one of life's deepest pains. Whether it's the death of a loved one, the end of a relationship, or the loss of a dream, grief can leave you feeling broken and hopeless. But even in the depths of sorrow, God offers His comfort and hope.

Revelation 21:4 paints a beautiful picture of the future God has promised—a time when pain and loss will be no more. This verse reminds us that the suffering we experience now is temporary and that God is working toward a glorious restoration. While this promise doesn't erase the pain, it can bring peace and hope to sustain you in the midst of grief.

God is near to the brokenhearted (Psalm 34:18), and He longs to comfort you in your pain. He understands your sorrow and invites you to bring your tears and burdens to Him. As you lean into His presence, He will give you the strength to take one step at a time, reminding you that you are not alone.

Loss can feel overwhelming, but God's love and comfort are greater. Trust Him to guide you through grief, and hold on to the hope that He is making all things new.

Reflect

- What loss are you grieving, and have you invited God into your healing process?
- How can remembering God's eternal promises help you find hope in the midst of sorrow?
- What practical ways can you experience God's comfort today?

Prayer

Lord, I bring my broken heart to You, trusting in Your promise to comfort and restore me. Help me to find hope in Your Word and to trust that You are working in ways I cannot see. Thank You for Your presence in my grief and for the promise of a future where there will be no more pain or loss. Give me strength to take each day one step at a time and to lean on Your everlasting love. In Jesus' name, Amen.

Action Step

Take time today to reflect on God's promises of comfort and restoration. Write down one way you've seen God's faithfulness in your life, even amid loss, and thank Him for His presence and love.

Promise to Hold On To

"The Lord is close to the brokenhearted and saves those who are crushed in spirit."
—Psalm 34:18

21

Day 21: Battling Negative Self-Talk

"We demolish arguments and every pretension that sets itself up against the knowledge of God, and we take captive every thought to make it obedient to Christ."
2 Corinthians 10:5

Negative self-talk can be one of the greatest battles you face. Thoughts like *"I'm not enough," "I'll never succeed,"* or *"I'm unworthy"* can fill your mind, leaving you feeling defeated and far from God's truth. But you don't have to live under the weight of those lies. God has given you the power to take every thought captive and make it obedient to Christ.

In 2 Corinthians 10:5, Paul encourages believers to demolish false arguments and align their thinking with God's Word. This is an intentional, active process. When a negative thought enters your mind, compare it to what God says about you. If it doesn't match His truth, replace it with what His Word declares. For example:

- Replace *"I'm not enough"* with *"I am fearfully and wonderfully made"* (Psalm 139:14).
- Replace *"I'll never succeed"* with *"I can do all things through Christ who strengthens me"* (Philippians 4:13).
- Replace *"I'm unworthy"* with *"I am chosen and dearly loved"* (Colossians 3:12).

Battling negative self-talk is not a one-time event—it's a daily surrender to God's truth. Meditate on Scripture, pray for wisdom, and trust God to renew your mind. As you align your thoughts with His Word, you'll experience freedom and peace.

Reflect

1. What negative thoughts do you often struggle with, and how do they impact your life?
2. How can Scripture help you combat the lies and replace them with God's truth?
3. What steps can you take today to intentionally guard your thoughts?

Prayer

Lord, I struggle with thoughts that tear me down and keep me from seeing myself as You see me. Help me to take every thought captive and make it obedient to Your truth. Remind me of who I am in You, and give me the strength to reject lies and embrace Your promises. Renew my mind, Lord, and let my thoughts glorify You. Thank You for Your truth that sets me free. In Jesus' name, Amen.

Action Step

Write down one negative thought you've been struggling with recently. Find a Bible verse that counters that thought with God's truth, and memorize it. Each time the negative thought arises, declare the Scripture over yourself.

Promise to Hold On To

"Do not conform to the pattern of this world, but be transformed by the renewing of your mind." —Romans 12:2

22

Day 22: Freedom from Guilt and Shame

"Therefore, there is now no condemnation for those who are in Christ Jesus."
Romans 8:1

Guilt and shame can weigh heavily on your heart, chaining you to past mistakes and making you feel unworthy of God's love. But Romans 8:1 reminds us of a powerful truth: if you are in Christ, there is no condemnation. Through Jesus' sacrifice, your sins are forgiven, and you are set free.

God's forgiveness isn't partial—it's complete. When He forgives, He separates your sins from you as far as the east is from the west (Psalm 103:12). Yet, even though God has forgiven you, it's often hard to forgive yourself. Guilt whispers, *"You're not good enough,"* and shame tries to define you by your past. But these voices are not from God.

God's love calls you to live in the freedom of His grace. His forgiveness wipes away your sin, and His mercy makes you new. When guilt or shame tries to pull you back, remind yourself of this truth: you are not defined by your mistakes but by your identity in Christ.

Let go of the weight of guilt and shame. Trust in God's forgiveness, and walk boldly in the freedom He has given you.

Reflect

- What guilt or shame from your past are you still holding onto?
- How does the promise of Romans 8:1 change the way you view yourself in Christ?
- What steps can you take to live in the freedom of God's forgiveness today?

Prayer

Lord, I thank You for Your forgiveness that sets me free. Help me to let go of guilt and shame and to trust that Your grace is enough. Remind me that I am not condemned and that my identity is found in You, not in my past mistakes. Teach me to live boldly in the freedom You have given me and to extend that grace to myself and others. In Jesus' name, Amen.

Action Step

Write down any guilt or shame you've been holding onto. After reflecting on God's forgiveness, tear up the paper as a symbol of releasing those burdens to Him.

Promise to Hold On To

"If we confess our sins, he is faithful and just and will forgive us our sins and purify us from all unrighteousness." —1 John 1:9

23

Day 23: Cultivating a Grateful Heart

"Give thanks in all circumstances; for this is God's will for you in Christ Jesus."
1 Thessalonians 5:18

In the rush of daily life, stress and worries often dominate your thoughts. Challenges at work, family pressures, or unexpected hardships can make it difficult to focus on anything other than what's wrong. But 1 Thessalonians 5:18 calls us to a higher perspective: to give thanks in all circumstances. Gratitude isn't about ignoring life's difficulties; it's about shifting your focus to God's goodness and faithfulness, even in the midst of challenges.

Cultivating a grateful heart starts with a decision. When stress or negativity creeps in, intentionally look for something to thank God for. It could be as simple as a moment of peace, a loved one's kindness, or the beauty of creation. Gratitude helps you see life through the lens of God's blessings rather than the weight of your problems.

As you practice thankfulness, you'll find that it changes your perspective. Stress begins to lose its grip as you focus on God's provision, and your heart becomes filled with His peace. Gratitude is a powerful tool that not only draws you closer to God but also transforms your outlook on life.

Reflect

- What situations in your life make it hard to feel grateful, and how can you find reasons to give thanks in them?
- How can shifting your focus to gratitude help you manage stress and anxiety?
- What blessings in your life are you most thankful for today?

Prayer

Lord, thank You for Your faithfulness in every season of my life. Teach me to cultivate a heart of gratitude, even when I'm facing stress or challenges. Help me to see Your hand at work in all circumstances and to trust in Your provision. Fill my heart with thankfulness that overflows into every area of my life. In Jesus' name, Amen.

Action Step

Start a gratitude journal. Write down three things you are thankful for today, no matter how small. Make this a daily habit to shift your focus to God's blessings.

Promise to Hold On To

"The Lord is my strength and my shield; my heart trusts in him, and he helps me. My heart leaps for joy, and with my song I praise him." —Psalm 28:7

24

Day 24: Pressing Through Burnout

"But those who hope in the Lord will renew their strength. They will soar on wings like eagles; they will run and not grow weary, they will walk and not be faint."
Isaiah 40:31

Burnout can leave you feeling empty, exhausted, and overwhelmed. Whether it stems from work, relationships, or the constant demands of life, burnout drains your energy and dims your joy. But Isaiah 40:31 offers a life-giving promise: when you place your hope in the Lord, He will renew your strength.

Renewal begins when you pause and rest in God's presence. Instead of striving to push through exhaustion on your own, bring your burdens to Him. Spend time in prayer and in His Word, allowing His peace to fill your heart. Like a weary traveler stopping at an oasis, find refreshment in His care.

God doesn't expect you to carry life's weight alone. He promises to give you the strength to keep going—not in your own power, but in His. Burnout is a reminder to release control and trust God to guide and sustain you. When you lean on Him, He lifts you up, enabling you to rise above your struggles and continue your journey with renewed purpose.

Reflect

- What signs of burnout are you experiencing, and have you brought them to God?
- How can resting in God's presence help you renew your strength?
- What practical changes can you make to create space for spiritual and physical rest?

Prayer

Lord, I feel weary and worn out from life's demands. I bring my exhaustion to You, trusting that You will renew my strength. Teach me to rest in Your presence and to rely on Your power rather than my own. Fill me with hope and peace as I press on, knowing that You are with me every step of the way. Thank You for being my source of strength and my refuge. In Jesus' name, Amen.

Action Step

Set aside 10–15 minutes today to rest in God's presence. Read Isaiah 40:28-31, and spend time in prayer or quiet reflection, asking God to renew your strength.

Promise to Hold On To

"Come to me, all you who are weary and burdened, and I will give you rest."
—Matthew 11:28

25

Day 25: God's Faithfulness Through Life's Storms

"Because of the Lord's great love we are not consumed, for his compassions never fail. They are new every morning; great is your faithfulness."
Lamentations 3:22-23

Life often brings storms—unexpected challenges, painful losses, or seasons of uncertainty. In those moments, it's easy to feel overwhelmed and question how you'll make it through. But even when life feels chaotic, God's faithfulness remains steadfast. His love is unfailing, and His mercies are new every morning.

Lamentations 3:22-23 was written during a time of great suffering, yet it proclaims the truth of God's unchanging faithfulness. No matter how fierce the storm, God's promises hold firm. He is your refuge, your strength, and your ever-present help in trouble (Psalm 46:1).

Clinging to God's promises during life's storms means trusting in His character, even when circumstances feel uncertain. Instead of focusing on the chaos around you, fix your eyes on the One who is in control. Pray for peace, meditate on His Word, and rest in His unchanging love. He is with you in the storm, guiding you and providing the strength you need to endure.

God's faithfulness has carried you through past challenges, and it will carry you through today's trials. Trust that He will see you through to calmer waters.

Reflect

- What storm are you currently facing, and how has it impacted your faith?
- How does remembering God's faithfulness in the past encourage you in the present?
- What Scripture or promise from God can you hold on to during this season?

Prayer

Lord, life feels chaotic right now, and I need Your strength and peace. Thank You for Your faithfulness, which never wavers. Help me to trust in Your promises and to cling to Your unchanging love. Calm the storm in my heart as I fix my eyes on You. Thank You for being my refuge and for walking with me through every trial. In Jesus' name, Amen.

Action Step

Take a few moments to write down three ways God has been faithful to you in the past. Keep this list where you can see it, and let it remind you of His presence and power as you navigate life's storms.

Promise to Hold On To

"The Lord is good, a refuge in times of trouble. He cares for those who trust in him." —Nahum 1:7

26

Day 26: Love and Boundaries

"Jesus replied: 'Love the Lord your God with all your heart and with all your soul and with all your mind.' This is the first and greatest commandment. And the second is like it: 'Love your neighbor as yourself.'"
Matthew 22:37-39

As Christians, we are called to love others, but love doesn't mean sacrificing your well-being or peace. Healthy relationships require boundaries. Boundaries are not walls to keep people out but guidelines to protect your heart, time, and energy so you can love others from a place of strength and wholeness.

Jesus taught us to love God first and foremost, and then to love others *as ourselves*. This implies that self-care and respect are integral to loving well. If you constantly overextend yourself, say yes to every demand, or allow others to take advantage of you, you risk burnout and resentment. Instead, trust God to give you the wisdom and courage to establish boundaries that reflect His love and truth.

Boundaries allow you to show grace without enabling harmful behaviors. They help you manage your time and resources wisely so you can honor God, love others, and take care of yourself. Remember, even Jesus withdrew to quiet places to rest and pray (Luke 5:16). Loving well means balancing compassion with wisdom and being led by the Holy Spirit.

Reflect

- Are there any relationships or situations where you need to establish healthier boundaries?
- How can setting boundaries help you love others more effectively?
- What steps can you take to protect your peace while still showing love and grace?

Prayer

Lord, help me to love others with Your grace and wisdom. Teach me to set healthy boundaries that honor You and protect the peace You've given me. Give me discernment to navigate challenging relationships and courage to communicate truth in love. Help me to love as You love—freely, wisely, and wholeheartedly. In Jesus' name, Amen.

Action Step

Identify one area in your life where you need to set or strengthen a boundary. Take a small step toward implementing that boundary, and pray for God's guidance in maintaining it with love and grace.

Promise to Hold On To

"Above all else, guard your heart, for everything you do flows from it." —Proverbs 4:23

27

Day 27: Building Relationships Rooted in Christ

"As iron sharpens iron, so one person sharpens another."
Proverbs 27:17

Relationships are a gift from God, meant to encourage, challenge, and strengthen us in our walk with Him. Proverbs 27:17 reminds us of the power of Christ-centered friendships—just as iron sharpens iron, godly relationships can refine and uplift us, keeping our faith vibrant and our hearts aligned with God's will.

Building relationships rooted in Christ requires intentionality. Surround yourself with people who encourage your spiritual growth and point you back to God's Word during difficult times. Likewise, be the kind of friend who listens, supports, and prays for others. True Christ-centered friendships aren't just about shared interests; they're about shared faith and the commitment to grow together in God's love.

If you're longing for deeper connections, start by bringing your desire to God in prayer. Ask Him to guide you to people who will help you grow spiritually. Invest time in cultivating these relationships through fellowship, honesty, and mutual encouragement.

In a world that often promotes surface-level connections, Christ-centered relationships provide a deeper foundation. They remind us that we're not walking this journey of faith alone—we're part of a community that strengthens and inspires us to be more like Christ.

Reflect

- Who in your life sharpens your faith and encourages your walk with Christ?
- How can you invest in relationships that draw you closer to God?
- Are there ways you can be a better friend to those in your life by pointing them to Christ?

Prayer

Lord, thank You for the gift of relationships that strengthen my faith and encourage my walk with You. Help me to be intentional in building Christ-centered friendships that reflect Your love and truth. Teach me to invest in others, to encourage them, and to be sharpened by their wisdom and faith. Surround me with people who inspire me to grow closer to You. In Jesus' name, Amen.

Action Step

Reach out to a friend or mentor who has positively influenced your faith. Thank them for their role in your spiritual growth, and spend time together in prayer or studying Scripture.

Promise to Hold On To

"Let us consider how we may spur one another on toward love and good deeds, not giving up meeting together, as some are in the habit of doing, but encouraging one another." —Hebrews 10:24-25

28

Day 28: Finding Purpose in Every Season

"For I know the plans I have for you," declares the Lord, "plans to prosper you and not to harm you, plans to give you hope and a future."
Jeremiah 29:11

Life is full of seasons—some joyful, others challenging, and some that seem uneventful. In each of these seasons, it's natural to question your purpose and wonder if God is truly at work. Jeremiah 29:11 reminds us that God's plans for us are always good, even when we can't see the full picture.

Finding purpose in every season begins with trusting that God is sovereign. Whether you're in a season of growth, waiting, or rebuilding, He is weaving everything together for your good (Romans 8:28). The moments that feel insignificant or painful are often the very times God is shaping your character and preparing you for what's next.

Instead of striving to make sense of everything, rest in the truth that God's timing and plans are perfect. Ask Him to reveal how you can honor Him in your current season—whether through serving others, deepening your relationship with Him, or simply being faithful in small tasks. Trust that even in the quiet or difficult times, He is at work, guiding you toward the hope and future He has promised.

No season is wasted in God's hands. Lean into His purpose for today, knowing He is faithful to complete the work He has begun in you.

Reflect

- What season of life are you currently in, and how is it shaping your faith?
- How can you trust God's plan even when the path ahead feels unclear?
- What steps can you take to find purpose in your current season?

Prayer

Lord, thank You for the promise that You have good plans for my life. Help me to trust You, even when I don't understand what You are doing. Teach me to find purpose in every season and to seek Your will in all that I do. Strengthen my faith as I wait on Your timing and remind me that You are always working for my good. In Jesus' name, Amen.

Action Step

Write down one way you see God's hand at work in your current season. Reflect on how you can embrace His purpose for today, even if it feels small or unclear.

Promise to Hold On To

"He has made everything beautiful in its time." —Ecclesiastes 3:11

29

Day 29: Sharing Your Story with Boldness

*"Praise be to the God and Father of our Lord Jesus Christ, the Father of compassion
and the God of all comfort, who comforts us in all our troubles, so that we can
comfort those in any trouble with the comfort we ourselves receive from God."*
2 Corinthians 1:3-4

Your story is powerful. Every trial you've faced, every victory you've experienced, and every moment you've felt God's presence has been woven into your life as a testimony to His goodness and faithfulness. Sharing your story isn't just about recounting what God has done for you—it's about encouraging others who are walking through their own struggles.

In 2 Corinthians 1:3-4, Paul reminds us that the comfort we receive from God is not meant to end with us. It's meant to overflow into the lives of others, offering hope and healing. By sharing your testimony, you shine a light on God's faithfulness and help others see that they're not alone.

It's natural to feel hesitant about sharing personal experiences, but remember that your story has value. The moments when you've felt weak, broken, or unsure are often the moments that God uses most powerfully to connect with others. Pray for boldness and trust that God will guide your words.

Your testimony is a reflection of His grace and redemption, a reminder that no matter how difficult life becomes, God is always present, working for good. Speak with confidence, knowing that your story has the power to inspire and encourage others in their faith journey.

Reflect

- How has God comforted or guided you in past trials, and how can you share that with others?
- Who in your life might be encouraged by hearing your testimony?
- What fears or hesitations might hold you back from sharing your story, and how can you overcome them?

Prayer

Lord, thank You for the ways You've worked in my life. Give me the courage to share my story boldly, knowing that it reflects Your faithfulness and grace. Help me to speak with humility and compassion, using my experiences to encourage others and point them to You. Use my testimony for Your glory and to bring hope to those who need it. In Jesus' name, Amen.

Action Step

Take time to write down your testimony, focusing on how God has worked in your life during specific challenges. Pray about who might need to hear it, and look for an opportunity to share it with someone in the coming week.

Promise to Hold On To

"They triumphed over him by the blood of the Lamb and by the word of their testimony." —Revelation 12:11

30

Day 30: Living a Life of Victory

"Brothers and sisters, I do not consider myself yet to have taken hold of it. But one thing I do: Forgetting what is behind and straining toward what is ahead, I press on toward the goal to win the prize for which God has called me heavenward in Christ Jesus."
Philippians 3:13-14

Living a victorious life in Christ doesn't mean life is free from challenges, but it does mean that through Christ, you can overcome every obstacle. Victory isn't about perfection or never stumbling; it's about pressing forward, keeping your focus on God, and trusting Him to guide you toward His eternal promises.

Paul's words in Philippians remind us to let go of the past—whether it's failures, regrets, or even past victories—and to keep straining toward what lies ahead. Life's race is not a sprint but a marathon, and running it well requires perseverance, discipline, and a fixed focus on Jesus. When setbacks arise, God's grace gives you the strength to stand up and keep moving forward.

Victory comes when you live with eternity in mind, making daily decisions that reflect your ultimate goal of glorifying God. As you press on, remember that Christ has already secured your victory through His death and resurrection. You are running from a place of victory, not for it. Keep your eyes on

Him and finish your race strong, knowing the eternal prize awaits you.

Reflect

- What past failures or distractions do you need to release to fully focus on God's purpose for your life?
- How does keeping your eyes on eternity change the way you face daily challenges?
- What practical steps can you take to run your race with perseverance and faith?

Prayer

Lord, thank You for the victory I have in You. Help me to let go of the past and keep my focus on the eternal prize You have promised. Give me strength to run my race with perseverance and grace, trusting You to guide me each step of the way. Let my life reflect Your glory and inspire others to seek You. In Jesus' name, Amen.

Action Step

Identify one area where you feel stuck or defeated. Surrender it to God in prayer and take a small step forward today, trusting in His strength and victory.

Promise to Hold On To

"In all these things we are more than conquerors through him who loved us." —Romans 8:37

31

Closing Reflection and Prayer

As you conclude this 30-day devotional journey, take a moment to reflect on the road you've traveled. Over the past month, you've explored themes of faith, trust, perseverance, and growth in your walk with God. Each devotion has been a step in nurturing your relationship with Him and discovering more of His purpose for your life. Now, as you prepare to step into what lies ahead, the call is to embrace a lifestyle of surrender and trust—living daily in God's presence and power.

Embracing a Lifestyle of Surrender and Trust

Surrender and trust are essential to a victorious Christian life, but they're not always easy. The world teaches us to be self-reliant, to pursue control, and to find validation in our achievements. Yet, God calls us to something far greater: a life marked by complete dependence on Him.

Surrendering to God means releasing the grip you have on your plans, fears, and expectations. It's acknowledging that His ways are higher than yours (Isaiah 55:8-9) and that His plans for you are always good, even when they don't align with your own (Jeremiah 29:11). Surrender isn't a one-time event; it's a daily decision to lay everything at His feet—your hopes, your struggles, your ambitions—and trust Him to lead you.

Trust is the fruit of surrender. When you truly believe in God's goodness and faithfulness, it becomes easier to rely on Him in every aspect of your life. Trust doesn't mean you'll never face uncertainty, but it does mean you can face it with peace, knowing that God is in control. He walks with you through every valley and celebrates with you on every mountaintop.

As you embrace surrender and trust, you'll find freedom. Freedom from the weight of trying to do it all on your own. Freedom from fear, worry, and the pressure to be perfect. You'll discover that God's grace is sufficient for your weakness (2 Corinthians 12:9) and that His power is made perfect in every area where you feel inadequate.

A Life Transformed by Surrender and Trust

Living a life of surrender and trust doesn't mean you won't face challenges. It means that when those challenges come, you'll respond differently. Instead of reacting with anxiety, you'll approach them with faith. Instead of clinging to control, you'll let God take the reins. Here are a few ways this lifestyle can transform your daily walk:

1. **Peace Amid Uncertainty**
   When you trust God, you don't have to have all the answers. You can rest in the assurance that He does, and His timing is perfect. Whether you're waiting for a breakthrough in your career, healing in a relationship, or clarity in your next steps, surrendering your timeline to Him brings a peace that surpasses all understanding (Philippians 4:7).

2. **Strength in Weakness**
   Surrendering your struggles to God allows His strength to shine through your weakness. When you let go of the burden of trying to fix everything yourself, you make room for His power to work in and through you.

3. **Joy in Every Season**
   Trusting God enables you to find joy, even in seasons of waiting or hardship. You can celebrate the growth that comes from trials, knowing that He is refining you and preparing you for greater things (James 1:2-4).

4. **Purpose in the Present**
   Surrendering control doesn't mean giving up; it means letting God guide

you to where you're meant to be. As you trust Him, you'll begin to see His purpose in your current season and live with intentionality and gratitude.

Committing to a Life of Growth in Christ

As this devotional draws to a close, it's important to recognize that the journey doesn't end here. Growth in Christ is a lifelong process. Each day is an opportunity to deepen your relationship with Him, to trust Him more fully, and to reflect His love to the world around you.

Here are some practical ways to continue growing in your faith:

1. **Stay Rooted in the Word**

   Make Scripture a part of your daily routine. Whether it's through a Bible reading plan, a devotional, or meditating on a single verse, God's Word is your foundation for growth.

2. **Cultivate a Heart of Prayer**

   Prayer is your direct line of communication with God. Bring Him your joys, your struggles, and your questions. Listen for His voice and let His Spirit guide you.

3. **Surround Yourself with Godly Community**

   Fellowship with other believers is essential for encouragement and accountability. Join a small group, attend church regularly, or find a mentor who can walk with you in your faith journey.

4. **Practice Surrender Daily**

   Begin each day by laying your plans and concerns before God. Ask Him to guide your steps and give you the strength to trust Him, even when things don't go as expected.

5. **Serve with Love**

   One of the best ways to reflect God's love is by serving others. Look for opportunities to be His hands and feet, whether in your family, your workplace, or your community.

Closing Prayer: Committing Your Journey of Faith to God

Heavenly Father,

Thank You for walking with me through this devotional journey. Thank You for the truths You've revealed, the encouragement You've provided, and the ways You've drawn me closer to You. Lord, I am so grateful for Your unfailing love and Your faithfulness in every season of my life.

As I move forward, I commit my journey of faith and growth to You. I surrender my plans, my fears, and my desires into Your hands, trusting that You will guide me in Your perfect way. Help me to live a life marked by surrender and trust, knowing that Your grace is sufficient for every challenge I face.

Lord, teach me to rest in Your peace when uncertainty arises. Remind me to seek You first in all that I do and to find my strength in Your promises. Let my life be a reflection of Your love, a testimony of Your faithfulness, and a beacon of hope to those around me.

Give me the courage to step boldly into the future You've prepared for me, and the humility to follow wherever You lead. As I continue this journey, may Your Word be a lamp to my feet and a light to my path.

Thank You, Lord, for the work You are doing in my heart and in my life. I trust You completely and commit myself to Your care. In Jesus' precious name, I pray, Amen.

The end of this devotional is the beginning of something new. As you step into the days ahead, remember that God is with you in every moment. He is your source of strength, your place of rest, and your ultimate hope. Embrace a lifestyle of surrender and trust, and watch as He transforms your life in ways you never imagined.

You are His beloved daughter, created for His glory and called to live a life of purpose. Walk confidently in His promises, knowing that the best is yet to come.